Why Is It So Hard to Breathe?

A FIRST LOOK AT ASTHMA

PAT THOMAS
ILLUSTRATED BY LESLEY HARKER

BARRON'S

Would you like to know something amazing? You breathe air in and out of your lungs thousands of times a day.

Most of the time breathing is so easy that we never have to think about it. But for some people breathing can sometimes be really hard. These people have asthma.

When a really bad asthma attack comes it can be frightening.

You may find yourself coughing or wheezing and gasping for air.

It may feel as if a giant is sitting on your chest, stopping you from getting any air in.

What about you?

What happens when you have an asthma attack?
What does it feel like to you when you can't breathe?

Asthma is a condition that makes it hard to get
enough air into and out of your lungs.

You can get it when you are an adult, but most people get it when they are very young.

Asthma is not
like a cold—you
can't catch it
from someone.

12

And you can't always tell just by looking whether another person has asthma. Most of the time people with asthma breathe just like everyone else.

When you first find out you have asthma,
you may feel worried and you may have
a lot of questions.

Your parents and your doctor will be able to
help you understand what causes your asthma
and what you can do to make it better.

Your doctor might give you a test. He or she may ask you to blow one big puff into a special tube.

This tube measures how much air you can blow out all at once. People with asthma blow out less air than other people.

If your doctor thinks you have asthma, he
or she might also give you some other tests to
see if you have any allergies that may
cause your asthma.

Although asthma can't be cured, there are lots of ways to control it. Your doctor might give you medicine in something called an inhaler.

With an inhaler you breathe medicine straight into your lungs.

Some inhalers are used in the morning to prevent attacks during the day.

Some you can carry with you to make it easier to breathe if you start to wheeze (have trouble breathing) during the day.

Lots of things can make asthma worse,
including allergies to things in the air.

dust   mold   smoke   pets' fur

feathers   traffic fumes   pollen

Cold weather and exercising without first
warming up your muscles can also make it worse.

Having a cold or being scared or unhappy
can also make your asthma worse.

What about you?

Do you know the things that make your asthma worse?
Are you good at avoiding them?

As you get older you will learn to keep away from the things that make your asthma worse.

You'll also learn to keep your inhaler with you and know when an attack is coming.

The people who care about
you—your parents, teachers
and friends—will also need
to learn about these things
to help you stay healthy.

Asthma can be a pain.
Sometimes it might feel as if
you can't do the fun things
everyone else does.

24

But people with asthma can do almost anything.

In fact, lots of famous sports people, singers,
and people you see on TV have asthma.

They've learned that as long as they take a bit of extra care, having asthma doesn't mean they have to miss out on anything fun. And pretty soon you will find that out for yourself, too!

HOW TO USE THIS BOOK

Whenever you talk to your child about health matters it's best to be honest, open, and positive. Tell your child that asthma can't always be cured (only about half of children who have asthma "grow out of it") but that medicine can help control the symptoms. Talk about the equipment your child may encounter, such as peak flow monitors, nebulizers, and different types of inhalers.

Be patient. Children in the four to seven age group will not fully understand their condition and cannot be expected to be in complete control of their environments in order to avoid all asthma triggers. At this age they will understand that they have lungs that help them breathe, that asthma makes breathing difficult, and that certain things make asthma worse. But they may still expose themselves to triggers and risks if they are part of a group or if an activity looks like fun. Likewise, they can understand and assist with medicines, but it is up to parents and other caregivers to provide help and supervision.

As early as you can, make sure your child learns to recognize the things that trigger an asthma attack, and reinforce the need to avoid these things. With a slightly older child, it is worth exploring alternative breathing techniques such as those used in yoga or the Buteyko method. These can help your child breathe more fully and can help calm breathing when he or she feels an attack coming on.

Different children react to asthma differently. It's important to tailor your approach to your child and to provide the right level of reassurance and empathy. As often as possible, help your child understand that while asthma can't be ignored, it doesn't mean that he or she can't live a normal life. You may wish to find out about famous people who have asthma and discuss them with your child to show your child that what people with asthma do and achieve in life isn't limited by their disease. While your child is coming to terms with asthma, encourage descriptive, feeling words to describe symptoms.

Communication with caregivers and teachers is the key. If your child has asthma you will need to work with other adults who may care for him or her so that everyone knows what triggers to avoid and what to do if the child has an attack. Make sure you know of any activities that might have an impact on your child's asthma. If you wish your child's health problems to remain confidential at school, this should be respected.

In school, learning about asthma can be covered through health education (how the lungs work and what allergies are, for instance) and also through science (e.g., understanding environmental triggers such as pollen). Many students may know about asthma: They may have it themselves or have a family member or friend with the condition.

An interesting way to get children who don't have asthma to understand what it feels like is to stage a simple exercise. Have the children run in place for one minute. They should be breathing hard and fast when they finish. When they stop, tell them to block their noses, put a straw in their mouths and close their lips around it, and then try to breathe through the straw (they should do this only for a few seconds). This will give them an indication of how hard it can be to get air into the lungs when the airways have closed up.

BOOKS TO READ

The ABC's of Asthma: An Asthma Alphabet Book for Kids of All Ages
Kim Gosselin and Terry Ravanelli (Jayjo Books, 1998)

The Lion Who Had Asthma
Jonathon London and Nadine Bernard Westcott
(Albert Whitman & Company, 1997)

Zoey and the Zones: A Story for Children with Asthma
Shawn R. McCormick, Ginny Trevino, and Nathan Schmidt (HealthSprings, 2002)

RESOURCES FOR ADULTS

American Academy of Allergy, Asthma & Immunology
555 East Wells Street
Suite 1100
Milwaukee, WI 53202-3823
(414) 272-6071
Patient Information and Physician
    Referral: 1-800-822-2762
www.aaaai.org

Allergy & Asthma Network Mothers of Asthmatics
2751 Prosperity Ave., Suite 150
Fairfax, VA 22031
Phone: 800-878-4403
Fax: 703-573-7794
www.aanma.org

Asthma and Allergy Foundation of America
1233 20th Street, NW
Suite 402
Washington, DC 20036
Hotline: 1-800-7-ASTHMA (1-800-727-8462)
www.aafa.org

Buteyko Institute of Breathing and Health
PO Box 3983
Manuka, ACT 2603
Australia
Tel: 011-61-3-9419-4211
www.buteyko.info
(Note that there are a limited number of practitioners in the U.S.)

BOOKS

Children with Asthma: A Manual for Parents, Thomas F. Plaut, M.D. (Pedipress, 1998)

The Complete Kid's Allergy and Asthma Guide: Allergy and Asthma Information for Children of All Ages (A Parent's Handbook), Milton Gold (Robert Rose Inc., 2003)

Guide to Your Child's Allergies and Asthma: Breathing Easy and Bringing Up Healthy, Active Children, Michael J. Welch, M.D. (American Academy of Pediatrics, 2000)